DRUGS
THE COMPLETE STORY

HEROIN

Mark Pownall

Robinson Township Public
Library District
606 N. Jefferson Street
Robinson, IL 62454

A Division of Steck-Vaughn Company

Austin, Texas

CONTENTS

GLOSSARY 4

1 OPIUM, MORPHINE, AND HEROIN 5

When sniffed, smoked, or injected, heroin makes most first-time users sick.

2 THE OPIUM POPPY 10

Opium is . . . the only drug used . . . in ancient times that is still used today in medicine.

3 THE POPPY FIELDS 15

The number of producers is almost limitless.

4 FROM POPPY TO POWDER 19

"They'll mix it with anything — mothballs, glucose, brick dust — anything."

CONTENTS

5 THE TRAFFICKERS 23

Heroin is now a global product traded, like coffee or sugar...

6 WHO USES HEROIN AND WHY 28

"If you need to score you'll do anything."

7 HEROIN ON THE STREETS 34

A once-wealthy Hollywood antique dealer... staged 64 bank robberies to pay for heroin costing him $800 a day.

8 THE COST TO HEALTH 39

Every year, two out of every 100 users of heroin will die.

9 THE SOCIAL COSTS 45

"You don't care about anybody."

10 KICKING THE HABIT 50

There is no magic cure for heroin.

11 WAR ON HEROIN 55

The problem for the health of society is that heroin is enormously profitable.

INFORMATION 61

INDEX 62

GLOSSARY

addiction: the forming of a dependence on a drug.
alkaloid: one of a group of substances found in the leaves of plants, that contain nitrogen, oxygen, carbon, and hydrogen. Morphine, cocaine, caffeine, and nicotine are all alkaloids.
cold turkey: the complete withdrawal from the use of an addictive drug.
CPR: a method of first aid used to restore breathing.
crack: the smokable form of cocaine, made by mixing cocaine hydrochloride with bicarbonate of soda in a laboratory.
detoxification program: a regime to help addicts give up heroin and expel the effects of the drug from their bodies.
diamorphine: the chemical term for pure heroin.
endorphins: the body's natural painkillers.
heroin base: the substance produced when morphine is mixed with acetic anhydride.
heroin salt: the addictive form of the drug, obtained after heroin base is treated chemically.
laudanum: a mixture of opium and alcohol.
mainlining: injecting heroin directly into a vein.
morphine: the very strong painkiller that is produced when opium is treated chemically.
opium: an impure substance that is obtained from the sap of the opium poppy.
pusher: someone who sells heroin and other drugs illegally.
score: street language for buying drugs.
skin-popping: injecting heroin into the skin.
withdrawal: the symptoms felt by a user who stops taking a drug after a period of addiction.
works: the needle and syringe an addict uses to inject heroin.

OPIUM, MORPHINE, AND HEROIN

Pure heroin is a white powder that is prohibited for medical use in the U.S. Heroin bought on the street is usually a dirty brown color and is far from pure, containing up to 95 percent of other substances such as chalk, sugar, or even brick dust. Both forms of heroin are highly addictive.

> *When it is sniffed, smoked, or injected, heroin makes most first-time users sick.*

Heroin comes from opium, a substance derived from the opium poppy, which is grown in three main areas of the world. These areas are Pakistan and Afghanistan in southwest Asia; the Laos, Thailand, Burma "golden triangle" in southeast Asia; and Mexico. Heroin is manufactured and smuggled all over the world, crisscrossing through complex routes to stay one step ahead of the customs officials whose job it is to prevent heroin from crossing international borders.

The users

When it is sniffed, smoked, or injected, heroin makes most first-time users sick. More experienced users get a "rush" that lasts for about a minute, then a feeling of sleepiness, and that everything is all right with the world, for about four hours. Heroin promotes this good feeling, while it lasts, by taking the place of some of the body's own natural painkillers. The brain has at least 15 of these natural painkillers, or endorphins, which help to keep it in a careful emotional balance. Heroin disturbs

HEROIN

Terraced opium fields make use of rugged landscape in northwest Pakistan.

this emotional balance by interfering with the endorphins.

Some of those users who are very dependent on the drug think of little else. Their life becomes a cycle of finding money by whatever means, buying some heroin, using the heroin, waiting for the effects to wear off, then trying to find more money for the next hit. One user described a typical day like this: "You get up, get your money, get your bag, inject it, watch some television, and wonder where the next bag is coming from."

Taking heroin every day for a period of weeks leads to dependence, or addiction, when the body needs heroin just to stay relatively normal. If the person who has become addicted to heroin stops taking the drug, he or she suffers withdrawal symptoms which resemble a bad case of the flu. Hundreds of thousands of people throughout the world are addicted to heroin, or to one of its close relatives such as opium.

In 1985 about 200,000 heroin addicts, or one-third of those in the U.S., lived in New York City alone. A total of 80 percent of U.S. addicts are divided equally between whites and blacks, with the remaining 20 percent either Hispanics or Orientals; about 25 percent are women. Most are young males in their twenties who started using heroin in their teens. While most are poor, there are many who are not.

OPIUM, MORPHINE, AND HEROIN

Opium and morphine

Opium is an impure substance that is derived from the sap of the opium poppy. It has been known for thousands of years and was used by the ancient Egyptians. In the nineteenth century, opium became a very important item of trade for the British in India. They exported the drug to China, where much of the population became addicted to smoking opium. The British fought two wars, the Opium Wars, to enable them to keep supplying China's opium addicts. This in turn meant that they could continue to make vast profits. The situation is similar today, except that those making the illegal profits are now the big heroin dealers. The big dealers are often a part of organized crime rings.

> *The British fought two wars, the Opium Wars, to enable them to keep supplying China's opium addicts. This in turn meant that they could continue to make vast profits.*

The drug morphine was purified from opium nearly 200 years ago, in 1803. Ninety years later, heroin was made from morphine. Heroin is much more efficient at getting into the brain than morphine, which is where both drugs have their

The British fought two wars against the Chinese over opium trading.

HEROIN

effects. Heroin is much stronger at killing pain and producing the initially pleasant feelings that addicts crave.

Heroin

Pure heroin (diamorphine) is used in some countries as a way of killing pain after accidents, after surgical operations, or when someone is suffering from pain caused by an illness such as cancer. It is one of the strongest painkillers available. Pure heroin is not, in itself, very harmful. According to some studies the nicotine in cigarettes is a more powerfully addictive drug and alcohol does much more long-term damage. The heroin taken by people who are dependent on the drug, however, is very different from clean, pure heroin.

The strength of heroin varies considerably, from about five to 50 percent purity or more. It is the substances that are added to heroin that cause much of the death and injury linked to the drug. Addicts always run the risk of taking so much that their breathing is slowed, sometimes so much that they die. This overdosing is usually caused by the fact that the user does not know exactly what has been mixed with the heroin, and how pure the drug that they are smoking or injecting actually is.

The reasons why people take heroin are many. For most it is

> Both men and women may sell their bodies for sex to get money to buy more drugs.

a mixture of pressure from friends and curiosity. Some use heroin as a way of escaping from anxiety, or because they feel lonely or unable to cope with life. Others take heroin simply because there is a lot of it around. Heroin is now much cheaper than it has been in the past, and sometimes cheaper than cocaine. This has meant that people who could not otherwise afford heroin have tried it and some have become addicted to it, or "hooked."

Addicts have to find money to buy heroin, which can be very expensive. It is difficult to find the money to pay for drugs by legal means. Many addicts steal from friends, family, cars, and their own and other people's houses, in order to buy drugs. Both men and women may sell their bodies for sex to get money to buy more drugs.

OPIUM, MORPHINE, AND HEROIN

Heroin addicts often live in poor housing or are homeless. Unhygienic conditions, such as the practice of sharing needles, frequently result in disease.

There are other dangers. Illegal drugs are often so impure that they have a terrible effect on those who take them. Addicts who pass needles and syringes to one another, even only once, run a high risk of passing on serious infections, including HIV, the AIDS virus.

"Giving up heroin is not easy. Surprisingly, though, 40 to 50 percent of those dependent on heroin do manage to give up the drug. Some do it by themselves or with the help of friends to relieve the symptoms of withdrawal. Some undergo a medically supervised treatment, or detoxification. Others find that the support of other addicts in organizations like Narcotics Anonymous is useful, and others find help in special communities and rehabilitation centers.

Heroin abuse is a problem that is growing. However, efforts to fight the spread of the drug have been largely unsuccessful. If the use of heroin is to be curbed, it is important that people understand the social and economic, as well as the mental and physical reasons, behind the use of heroin.

THE OPIUM POPPY

Heroin is made from the white opium poppy, one of a family of 250 different types of poppy that grow all over the world. The opium poppy is an annual plant and new seeds need to seed themselves or be planted each year. In the right conditions, the plants grow up to two feet high within two months. The flowers do not last long, and a seed pod the size of a golf ball develops. It is this seed pod that is the source of the crude opium used to make heroin.

An ancient remedy

The first records of opium being used date from more than 6,000 years ago. Egyptian priests used opium as part of their religious ceremonies. There is evidence that it was used for the same purposes in other parts of the Middle East.

Seeds and seedheads of the opium poppy have been found by archaeologists digging up the remains of a community of Stone Age lake-dwellers who lived in Switzerland 4,000 years ago. These remains probably show that this community, which had not developed a means of reading and writing, had found out about the effects of opium.

> *Opium is perhaps the only drug used by doctors in ancient times that is still used today in medicine.*

Opium is perhaps the only drug used by doctors in ancient times that is still used today in medicine. Doctors at the early centers of medicine in Egypt and Persia (present-day Iran)

THE OPIUM POPPY

Heroin is derived from the attractive opium poppy flower.

were treating patients with opium before 200 B.C. The use of the drug spread from Egypt to the rest of the Middle East, and then to the great ancient civilization of Greece.

The Roman empire, which extended far and wide into North Africa and northern Europe, as well as all around the Mediterranean Sea, adopted many things from the ancient Greeks, including opium. The Roman poet Virgil (70 –19 B.C.) mentions the use of the drug to bring on sleep. The greatest doctor in ancient Rome was Galen, who lived in the second century A.D., when he was doctor to the emperor Marcus Aurelius. Galen was an enthusiastic user of opium mixtures.

Opium was popular among the Romans. It was sold in corner shops by ordinary shopkeepers, and by unqualified doctors or "quacks" who traveled around falsely promising that it would cure everything. In this, ancient Rome was similar to the United States in the nineteenth century, when "medicine men" traveled around selling panaceas, or cure-all medicines.

Over the following centuries opium was spread far and wide, especially by Arab traders who took the drug to India and China. Arab doctors made a special study of opium and recommended it especially for eye diseases and diarrhea. One

HEROIN

A drug jar from Iran, made about 1600, to hold theriac, or "Venice Treacle," an ancient medicine composed largely of opium.

famous Arab doctor, Avicenna, is thought to have been addicted to the drug and probably died from an overdose in 1037.

The expansion of Arab power in the tenth and eleventh centuries spread opium use even farther. Soldiers returning from the Crusades brought back knowledge of the drug to Europe. By the 1500s, opium was perhaps the most important part of the doctor's medicine chest and was found in most of the common mixtures made for specific conditions.

The opium eaters

Three hundred years ago in England, Dr. Thomas Sydenham developed the mixture of alcohol and opium that became known as laudanum. This became the cause of widespread addiction. Addiction to opium and the existence of withdrawal symptoms were recognized as early as 1700, but without the sort of alarm that has surrounded later scares. Taking opium was viewed as unusual and exotic. It was thought of chiefly as a habit that was derived from the East.

THE OPIUM POPPY

In the eighteenth and nineteenth centuries the first widespread problems of addiction to opium became apparent in China. Since 1757, British merchants had been exporting Indian opium from India to China, where it was smoked in opium dens. The traders exploited every link in the distribution chain, as top heroin traffickers do today, from cultivation to sale. For the first time opium became an important international product with great profits at stake.

> By the 1500s, opium was perhaps the most important part of the doctor's medicine chest.

Opium smoking greatly increased in China as a result of this efficient trade. In 1839 alone, 40,000 chests of opium were shipped to China. The effect of all this opium on so many of his people worried the emperor, who decided to try to stop the widespread addiction. He arrested opium dealers at the port of Canton and made ships carrying opium return to India.

The British government responded to protests from the traders and began the first of two Opium Wars by sending a fleet of ships "to punish the Chinese and restore free trade." The British forced the Chinese to legalize the opium trade in 1858 in an agreement that led to a soaring rate of addiction in China. By 1879 there were opium dens in nearly every town in China supplied from the 105,000 chests of opium sold by the British.

> The result was a serious breakdown in social order, and terrible levels of poverty and misery, as money and energy were devoted to smoking opium.

The result was a serious breakdown in social order, and terrible poverty and misery, as money and energy were devoted to smoking opium. In the early 1900s, though, public opinion against the opium trade mounted, and eventually Britain stopped selling opium to the Chinese. By this time there was an opium problem within Britain as well.

A campaign in Britain against opium warned against opium dens in the East End of London. However, the campaign ignored the availability of opium in pharmacies and corner

HEROIN

shops. Opium dens *were* dirty but quiet places, not the dens of "abominable sin" portrayed by campaigners and writers.

The campaign had its effect. In the 1850s, opium could be bought at any corner shop, but by the early 1900s, the sale of the drug had been restricted to pharmacies only. By 1912, there was an international agreement to limit the opium trade, and this was the start of international action to combat addiction to opium and related drugs. It has led to today's campaigns against heroin that have been launched by groups like the World Health Organization and customs authorities.

The use of opiates is not a new problem in this country. In the U.S., between 1830 and 1870, opiate "medicines" were popular home remedies. Morphine was freely used as a painkiller during the Civil War. In the 1850s and 1860s, tens of thousands of Chinese laborers entered the U.S. and brought with them the custom of smoking opium; racist sentiments were expressed against the Chinese for spreading addiction. During the late 1800s, morphine was easily obtained at any pharmacy. Soon, heroin was available. In 1920, there were a reported 300,000 morphine or heroin addicts in New York City. Finally, in 1924 Congress made the use of heroin illegal. Antidrug campaigns focused on the criminality of addiction.

The opium dens of London's East End had a reputation, exaggerated by popular nineteenth-century writers, for being places of mystery and evil.

THE POPPY FIELDS

The opium poppy grows well in climates that provide plenty of warmth and rain. Seeds from the poppy seed capsules are plentiful and germinate easily, which makes it difficult to reduce opium production. The number of producers is almost limitless. When production in one area is stopped, opium growers can simply move to another area to maintain production.

An easy crop

The opium poppy grows to a height of between 20 and 60 inches and has a single flower that is about three to five inches across when open. The flower is usually white, though it may be pink, red, or purple. The colors help officials to identify areas under opium poppy cultivation from aerial or satellite photographs.

> *The number of producers is almost limitless. When production in one area is stopped, opium growers can simply move to another area to maintain production.*

In Pakistan and Afghanistan there is often one sowing in the autumn and one in the spring. Sometimes the autumn crop is a partial failure because of bad weather or pests. The first crop flowers from the end of May to the beginning of June and the second crop starts about two weeks later.

Most heroin is derived from three main areas of the world: the "golden triangle" of Laos, northern Thailand, and Burma;

HEROIN

Farmers at Kohat Pass, Pakistan, gather opium. They work across the field, cutting every seed pod to get out the opium-bearing sap.

the "golden crescent" of the Pakistan-Afghanistan-Iran area controlled by a tribe called the Baluchi; and the western part of Mexico, which is the principal supplier to the U.S. Since the late 1970s these areas have increased their yields of poppies. The Pakistan-Afghanistan area produces more opium per acre than the other two areas because of the suitability of the soil and the better climate.

Profit and loss

Western governments sometimes fail to disrupt opium growing if it is being done by groups with which they are politically sympathetic. In the early 1980s, anti-Soviet tribesmen in Afghanistan were able to fund purchases of military equipment from profits made by the growth of poppies. Little was done to stop them.

Opium and heroin are an important source of income for many developing countries that have enormous debts. They are addicted to heroin in their own way — they cannot afford to stop growing it. None of the countries mentioned officially approves of the growing of poppies to produce heroin in their

THE POPPY FIELDS

countries. However, those who control the growing of opium poppies are wealthy and often in positions of great power.

The tens of thousands of poor peasant farmers who grow opium often have little reason to grow other crops. They earn far more for growing opium than they would if they grew food crops. Opium is an important "cash crop" that is sold to buy other goods.

One acre of opium poppies can produce about three pounds of opium. However, the peasant farmer will get less than five percent of the street price of heroin. The farmers themselves receive little of the massive profit that the illicit drug's trade produces. It is the refiners, smugglers, and traffickers who make most of the money.

Moreover, the farmer himself may be an addict, for it is not only people in Western countries who become addicted to opium and heroin. The hill farmers of Southeast Asia are themselves consumers of raw opium. They will often use a ball of opium during the long journeys they have to make. It is estimated that one million people in Pakistan out of a total population of 10 million are addicted to heroin, compared to the estimated 600,000 addicts in the U.S., which has a population of 250 million.

When the opium sap has dried into latex, it is gathered into a ball and tied in poppy leaves.

17

HEROIN

A profitable business

The growing and distribution of opium for manufacture into heroin is against the law (although some heroin is made for legal medical purposes outside the U.S.). This means that the exact size of the annual production of heroin is not known.

In many opium-growing countries the production of the drug is controlled by organized crime and local warlords who are ruthless and violent. The opium fields of Burma are home to Khun Sa, the world's biggest heroin dealer, who harvests 1,200 tons of raw opium for conversion to 120 tons of heroin. He has a private army of over 5,000 regular troops and the Burmese army generally leaves him in peace.

> "The corruption is unbelievable — they are clearly stopping trucks, seizing the heroin, and selling it back."

The influence of such organized crime extends to everyone, from the grower to the officials who are supposed to stop the trade. "The corruption is unbelievable — they are clearly stopping trucks, seizing the heroin, and selling it back," claims one World Health Organization drug official in Pakistan. Unfortunately, Khun Sa's is only one of many hundreds of drug organizations.

Many of the 5,000 soldiers in the army of the drug baron Khun Sa are very young boys. Khun Sa is the world's biggest heroin dealer.

FROM POPPY TO POWDER

Below the flowers of the opium poppy there is a bulge which is the seed capsule. Each plant contains five to eight flowers, and so the same number of capsules are formed. Each capsule contains a small amount of opium, which needs to be extracted and purified before it becomes heroin. When the unripe capsules of the opium poppy are cut, a white liquid oozes out. It is this liquid, or latex, which when dried is known as opium.

Harvesting

When the capsules are about one and a half inches across and the color is about to change from green to yellow, the poppy capsules are cut. This is usually done between midday and evening to get as much opium as possible. The cutters work in lines. After cutting in an area, they do not go back through that area again until the liquid from the capsule has had time to dry. They do this to avoid brushing against the poppies they have already cut and shaking off the liquid oozing out of the capsule onto the ground. The same problem can occur if it is raining or very windy, when the liquid can be shaken or washed off by the wind or rain.

Different knives are used in different places, but one kind that is used has seven small blades. The knife is run around the capsule in the same way as some people might cut around the skin of a baked apple before putting it into the oven. In other places, an instrument with several iron spikes is used to produce cuts down the poppy capsule. The cuts must be gentle. If they are too hard the liquid will run into the middle of the capsule and will be lost. This cutting process may take place several times over two or three days.

HEROIN

The poppy seed heads have to be split very carefully to allow the sap to run out. Special knives with several blades are used, like this one from Thailand.

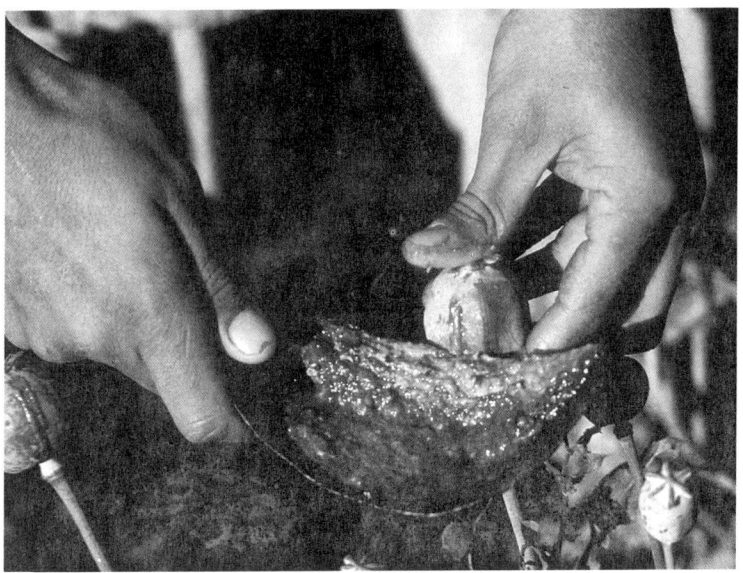

The white sap turns to latex as it dries and also darkens to brown. The brown latex is scraped off with a wide-bladed knife and dried further.

FROM POPPY TO POWDER

The liquid is then dried, either by leaving the capsules in the sun or by heating them artificially. The heat causes any water to evaporate, leaving the latex behind. The liquid latex starts off-white in color, but then it becomes solid and turns a muddy brown color. The opium poppies are left overnight after the cutting procedure and early the following morning the latex is scraped off using special knives or scrapers. Traditionally, ordinary knives are used and the opium is collected on a poppy leaf.

> The cuts must be gentle. If they are too hard the liquid will run into the middle of the capsule and will be lost.

Then the opium, which is still a little wet, is dried again. It is then formed into lumps and surrounded by poppy leaves. The moist opium may be left for several months to become even drier.

While opium is the main crop from the poppy seed, it is not the only one. The seeds can be pressed hard, and the oil that comes out can be used as a cooking oil. What is left is often used to feed cattle.

From opium to heroin

Opium is a natural plant product and contains a great many chemicals. These include sugars and salts, protein, coloring matter, and water. However, the most important chemicals are the 25 or so alkaloids, which are the elements of the plant product that react with the body to give a drug's effect. These nitrogen-containing chemicals are also found in morphine, the common painkiller codeine, and other prescription painkillers used by doctors, such as thebaine and papaverine.

> Opium is treated chemically to yield morphine . . . one of the most powerful painkillers known.

Opium is treated chemically to yield morphine, often very near to where the opium poppies are grown. Morphine is one of the most powerful painkillers known. It is used by doctors to help people who are in intense pain.

HEROIN

Morphine can be converted into heroin by mixing it with a highly reactive substance called acetic anhydride to form heroin base. This heroin base is then further treated to produce heroin salt. The addictive form of the drug is this salt rather than the base. Morphine is ten times stronger than opium and heroin is 25 times more powerful than opium.

Not so pure

Heroin salt is the substance that is smuggled all over the world. However, the heroin sold on the street is usually a very different substance from the pure white chemical that is first manufactured. Street heroin is mixed with all kinds of powders which range from harmless to lethal. Adding something cheap to expensive heroin, called "cutting it," is a good way for drug dealers to make extra profits, and it happens at every stage from large-scale suppliers to local addicts. As the heroin goes down the chain, it becomes ever more expensive and ever less pure.

> "They'll mix it with anything . . . mothballs, glucose, brick dust — anything."

This practice of mixing heroin with other substances is so common that police think they have caught a major supplier if what is seized contains more than 50 percent heroin. What addicts buy may have as little as 10 percent heroin. Exactly what people put in varies from place to place. Quinine is often mixed in with heroin sold on the streets of New York, while other drug mixtures are more common in Europe.

Many of the substances introduced are not drugs — talcum powder, sugar, glucose, and baking powder are also used. Occasionally even brick dust or household detergents are added: "They'll mix it with anything — mothballs, glucose, brick dust — anything." These substances can cause health problems and sometimes death.

THE TRAFFICKERS

Heroin is traded throughout the world by those who care little about the effect of their trade on addicts. The traditional trade routes meant that the U.S. received most of its heroin from Mexico, Australia received most of its supply from the golden triangle of Southeast Asia, and Europe received its heroin from Pakistan and Afghanistan. Today, the situation is very different. Heroin is now a global product traded, like coffee or sugar, around the clock and around the world.

> *Heroin is now a global product traded, like coffee or sugar, around the clock and around the world.*

Heroin is traded in all directions at once in order to stay one step ahead of customs and police officials. It is an international currency used by migrants and exiles, criminals and arms dealers. Heroin dealing is used to get around restrictions on the movement of money from country to country.

The smugglers

Heroin is sold by the farmer to the manufacturer who purifies it in factories. Then it is passed to the smuggler, on to the wholesaler and to the small dealer; then to even smaller dealers, who are probably drug addicts themselves. It is a complex flow that involves many people. However, the people who are most likely to be caught — those dealing heroin in the back alleys and the dirty front rooms of vandalized apartments — are least likely to know who the big dealers are.

HEROIN

Heroin laboratories are often secretly set up in houses, such as this one in Hong Kong. Heroin is distilled from morphine by a simple process and is 30 to 80 times more powerful.

The big dealers keep it that way by ruthlessly using violence against those who inform the police of their activities.

With increasing global travel and communication, it is becoming harder to stop the heroin trade. The flow of passengers at busy ports at peak times means that perhaps one in 100 are stopped. In the U.S., where 250 million people cross its borders each year, thorough searching of cars, ships, boats, and planes would bring unacceptable daily chaos to the lives of law-abiding international business people. The U.S. also has thousands of miles of borders, and hundreds of private airfields that are not guarded at night.

At Dover, in England, the most important port dealing with traffic between the U.K. and the rest of Europe, customs officers have an average of 45 seconds to search a car. To do the job properly, even without dismantling the car, would take an hour.

However, most heroin is transported around the world in cargo, in trucks, boats, and in airfreight. There is just not enough time to search all the cargo thoroughly. If officials at

THE TRAFFICKERS

any border tried to do that the delays would be intolerable and international trade would be impossible. Blocking trade and preventing freedom of movement might stop some heroin trafficking, but it would hinder innocent passengers.

Much of the heroin trade does not even have to run the risk of going through a customs examination. Bribes are a way of life in the heroin trade. When the street price of heroin is more than 300 times its original price, there is plenty of money to smooth the way with corrupt officials. Airport and dock workers are key targets for the heroin traders.

Some customs officials, in North America, Europe, and Australia, as well as Asia and Africa, earn large sums of money by turning a blind eye to certain pieces of baggage. Baggage handlers also are encouraged to "misroute" marked items of baggage so that they do not have to pass through customs, and cleaning people collect packets that have been hidden in bathrooms or garbage bags.

When Andreas Stathopoulos was captured in Greece in 1987, he was attempting to smuggle 50 pounds of heroin in his luggage.

HEROIN

Even heroin seized by police or customs can be stolen back by heroin dealers. In 1983, a gang made a violent attempt to break into and rob a customs shed at London's Heathrow airport that contained several million dollars' worth of drugs. In 1989, in South Australia, a corrupt head of the drug squad began serving a 28-year prison sentence for selling huge quantities of confiscated drugs, including heroin, back onto the streets. The U.S. Drug Enforcement Agency holds stocks of heroin and cocaine worth twice as much as the gold reserve held at Fort Knox.

Bribes are a way of life in the heroin trade.

The trade can also flourish by using little-known ports. Private aircraft, yachts, and fishing boats carry millions of dollars' worth of heroin and land at private airstrips and remote beaches without anyone noticing. There are frequent reports of boats being stopped and searched along the east coast of the United States. Many others are never detected.

The dealers

Both the appearance and status of dealers can be surprising. The big dealers look like conventional successful business people and would be at home in the financial centers of Wall Street or London. These people are highly organized and well financed. They have specialized equipment on the boats or planes used for smuggling that can detect any movement by customs officials and coastguard patrols.

The Mafia has established links with corrupt officials in Southeast Asia and is heavily involved in Latin American drug production.

Refinement and distribution of drugs in both North America and Europe is largely controlled by the Mafia, the organized crime syndicate. The Mafia's international drug trade is worth billions and billions of dollars; it is organized and maintained like a large but secret corporation. The Mafia was originally

THE TRAFFICKERS

In Southeast Asia, serious attempts to control drug trafficking are being made. These New Zealanders were captured by the Malaysian police in April 1989.

based in Sicily and has links with many powerful and seemingly respectable businessmen throughout the U.S., Canada, and Italy. To give some idea of the scale of the Mafia drug operation, one syndicate alone was equipped with 200 aircraft.

The Mafia has established links with corrupt officials in Southeast Asia and is heavily involved in Latin American drug production. Those who question the working of the Mafia are often subject to violence and murder. Politicians, judges, and journalists have all been killed for trying to discover what really goes on behind the Mafia's code of silence.

The sophistication of the trade in drugs carried out by organized crime can be seen in the deal worked out between the Gambino crime family in New York and the Fidanzati brothers of Milan, Italy. The deal exchanged heroin refining facilities in Italy for cocaine imported from the U.S. The families traded in drugs as if it were currency, with an exchange rate of three kilograms of cocaine for one kilogram of heroin. The profits were so great that the warring factions of Mafia-style organized crime buried their differences and cooperated with each other. However, experts believe that these "families" are not the ones that control most of the heroin trade. Their arrest in 1988 has not made a significant difference in the trafficking of the drug.

WHO USES HEROIN AND WHY

Once heroin has been smuggled into a country it soon finds its way into the hands of dealers in all major cities and many large towns, and then onto the streets. Who exactly is it, though, who buys heroin?

The users

Most surveys show that regular users of heroin are young, mainly between the ages of 16 and 24, and three out of four are male. In urban areas a high proportion of users, 80 percent, are unemployed. How the drug is taken varies and can change rapidly. For example, in Liverpool, England, the number of people injecting heroin in the years 1985 to 1988 has increased from 12 to 40 percent.

> "I had to move out of my home because I stole from my dad. I live in an apartment with nothing in it now. I felt ashamed and embarrassed about stealing from my dad, but I had to score. If you need to score you'll do anything. I haven't seen my parents since."

The reasons why people start to use heroin are often very different from the reasons why they use drugs in the long term. People start to use heroin for many reasons, including curiosity, simply because it is available, because their friends are encouraging them to try it, to be in fashion, to change how they feel, out of boredom, or to be rebellious and challenge authority. Some people, like this user, take heroin because they

WHO USES HEROIN AND WHY

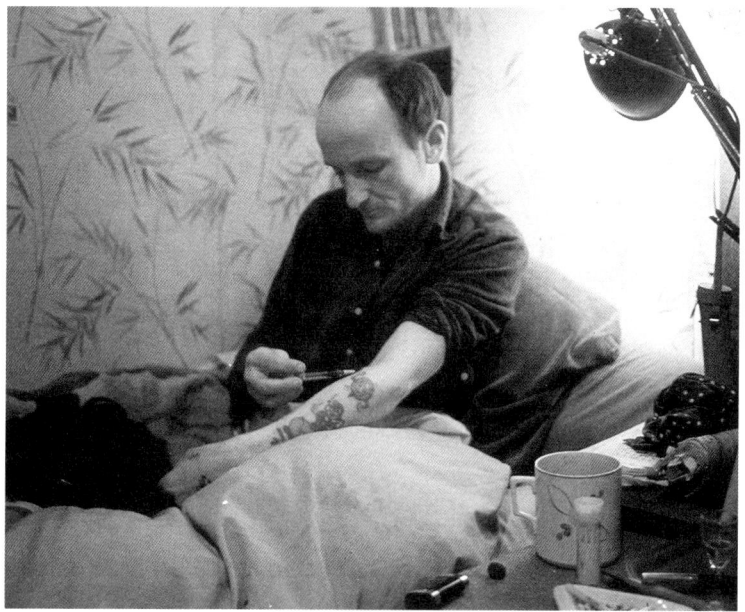

People start taking heroin for many different reasons. Once addicted, getting their next "hit" is the most important thing in their lives.

are depressed: "I'd just broken up with my girlfriend and I was really down. I took some heroin and all my worries just seemed to float away. I suppose I could have gotten back together with her, but I just wasn't thinking about her or anything else once I got hooked."

Teenagers especially want to try out new experiences as part of their development. This sometimes leads them to experiment with heroin. While most then give up the drug, some become addicted, and begin to harm themselves with the use of heroin. Many are like this 20-year-old addict who gave up everything for his habit: "I had to move out of my home because I stole from my dad. I live in a pad with nothing in it now. I felt so ashamed and embarrassed about stealing from my dad, but I had to score. If you need to score you'll do anything. I haven't seen my parents since."

Most addicts take heroin for the first time as the result of the encouragement of someone they know, and not from the "evil pushers" as portrayed by the media. Pushers are usually not strangers, but are often friends or family of the people they encourage to get hooked on heroin.

HEROIN

People are influenced by many things — by what they read, by travel to new and interesting places, by exercise and sports, by religion, and by building close emotional relationships. Heroin provides an artificial change in mood that may replace these comparatively harmless, natural changes of mood. The high price paid for the temporary lift given by heroin is addiction.

The reasons why people use heroin over a long period of time are more complex. Some continued use of heroin is an attempt to cope with a life without a job or other sources of interest and excitement. Others like to give themselves an identity by "labeling" themselves so they can at least claim: "I am a junkie." Other addicts may find it hard to like themselves or have problems relating to their families, and many come from unhappy homes where there is little love or affection, or where the addict feels rejected or angry.

> *Heroin's "high" is, in fact, a depression of the nervous system. For a while the drug dulls physical and mental pain and causes sleepiness. It reduces fear and anxiety and brings on a temporary feeling that everything is all right.*

Some experts believe that there is no such thing as an "addictive personality," that is, someone who is at much greater risk of becoming addicted to heroin and other drugs than most other people. Some addicts do, however, seem to share certain traits. They may be depressed and act as if they were younger than they really are. They may find it difficult to cope with being angry, or resent people they think are not on their side. Addicts may not feel good about themselves and may rebel against or lash out at any form of authority, like teachers, parents, and the police.

Heroin and the human body

Heroin is an artificially produced drug, but it is similar in structure to that group of natural substances, the endorphins, that act as the body's own painkillers. When heroin is injected, smoked, or sniffed, it is rapidly changed in the body into substances, similar to morphine, that are very active in the body. These metabolites, as they are called, fit into places in

WHO USES HEROIN AND WHY

the brain where the natural endorphins normally fit, just like a key in a lock. The effects of heroin are very crude compared to endorphins.

Different drugs related to heroin fit in different "locks" and produce slightly different effects, but all of them can cause dependence. This helps to explain why a heroin user will use codeine or other drugs related to heroin, if heroin itself is unobtainable.

Heroin's "high" is, in fact, a depression of the nervous system. For a while the drug dulls physical and mental pain and causes sleepiness. It reduces fear and anxiety and brings on a temporary feeling that everything is all right. For the four to eight hours that the effects of the drug last, the heroin user is calm. He or she thinks and moves slowly and generally feels lazy and peaceful.

At first a relatively small amount of the drug has this effect, but soon the body begins to become dependent. Regular users of heroin have to increase the dosage they take to achieve the same effect. Those dependent on heroin who have to take ever increasing doses are said to have developed a "tolerance" to the drug. A drug tolerance happens not just with heroin but with related opiate drugs and is caused by a need for more drugs to produce the effects of that drug. An addict with a high tolerance who overestimates his dose can easily overdose and die.

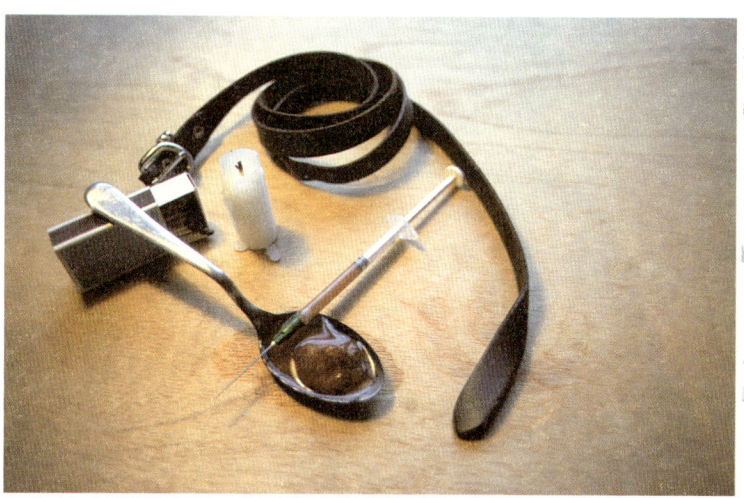

These are examples of the syringe, drugs, and other implements used to inject heroin. They are known as "works."

HEROIN

A privileged background

Jenny lived in an attractive suburb in an affluent area of the country. Her father worked hard and had a small but prosperous business. They lived a comfortable life in a large house; there was always plenty of money to buy almost anything that Jenny wanted.

At the age of 17, Jenny moved out of her parents' home to live with her boyfriend, Jim. Jim was a heroin addict, as Jenny soon learned, and after a while, she too began to take the drug. "I was determined never to touch heroin, and my boyfriend was equally determined that I wouldn't. Yet after my first big fight with my parents, it wasn't long before I had my first fix. The others were all using. I felt left out. The whole crowd was very involved with heroin."

> *"The others were all using. I felt left out. The whole crowd was very involved with heroin."*

Jenny paid for heroin by selling presents her parents had given her and, when that source of cash came to an end, by stealing from her former home. Her parents were outraged, but it was not until Jim died of an overdose that Jenny realized that she needed help. She made the decision to enter a drug treatment program run by ex-addicts. At the treatment center, there are no drugs, not even cigarettes or alcohol, and there is a simple lifestyle in which everything is shared.

Jenny came from a privileged background, but that did not stop her from getting caught in the heroin trap. It is difficult to know exactly why she started, but she received little love at home, for all her luxurious lifestyle, and her parents never seemed very interested in what she was doing. Jim loved and understood Jenny, but by being with him and his friends, Jenny felt pressured into taking heroin.

Heroin can be deadly

Darren was born into a poor Bronx neighborhood in New York. He grew up in an atmosphere where hustling was one way of getting your next meal. Since his early teens he had hardly ever gone to school but had hung around with older boys and had joined one of the city's street gangs. He began to run errands

WHO USES HEROIN AND WHY

In New York, many young addicts act as runners and street dealers for the drug traffickers. Like this boy, they are often arrested but usually released quickly.

for a local drug dealer, and it was not long before he took some heroin for himself.

Soon he was injecting, a real hazard in a city where it is difficult to obtain clean needles and syringes, called by addicts "works." "Everyone was using heroin and I joined in. You can't get needles without a prescription. You have to share. I didn't think the people I shared with would have the virus, but one of them must have."

Darren was injecting himself in so-called shooting galleries, where addicts gather to buy drugs and share needles and syringes. He was also stealing to pay for his addiction; he took handbags and wallets, and shoplifted as well as commiting some burglaries. However, he was not very successful.

He had felt ill for a while when he went to a doctor about a cough and a skin infection. The doctor took a sample of his blood, and this showed that he was one of the estimated 100,000 I.V. drug users who have tested positive with the AIDS virus.

33

HEROIN ON THE STREETS

Heroin is usually sold on the streets in bags containing enough brown powder for one fix. That means that four to eight hours after a fix, the effect of the drug wears off and the addict is out looking to buy, or "score," some more. An addict's life goes around in a seemingly endless circle, and its center is based on acquiring heroin.

Using heroin

Heroin may be sniffed, smoked, or injected. Swallowing it does not have much effect because it is broken down quickly by the liver. Heroin can be sniffed directly, like snuff. However, this is the way those dependent on drugs usually take cocaine; addicts are often dependent on more than one drug.

> It is sometimes thought that it is impossible to become dependent on heroin if the drug is smoked. This is not true.

Particularly in the U.K. smoking heroin, referred to as "chasing the dragon" or "Chinesing," is a common way to take heroin. When smoked, heroin, like the nicotine in cigarettes, enters the bloodstream very fast. Chasing the dragon involves putting the drug on a piece of tin foil and heating it with a match. The heroin blackens and wriggles like a snake and produces fumes that are inhaled.

It is sometimes thought that it is impossible to become dependent on heroin if the drug is smoked. This is not true. Smoking heroin every day for two or three weeks will produce

34

HEROIN ON THE STREETS

Particularly in the U.K., smoking heroin is often called "chasing the dragon." As the heroin is heated on a piece of foil, it blackens and wriggles while producing smoke, like a dragon.

a physical dependence on the drug. It becomes difficult to stop using it, even if the user wants to.

Recent medical research shows that smoking heroin causes chronic bronchitis and emphysema. It probably causes lung cancer too, though this is difficult to prove because most heroin addicts also smoke cigarettes.

> *Those who are seriously addicted to heroin will also inject their feet, neck, and legs.*

The third method of taking heroin has many hazards, including the risk of contracting AIDS. Addicts often add an acid to heroin to make it easier to inject, and there are several different ways of injecting the drug. If it is injected into the skin, it is known as "skin-popping." "Mainlining" is when heroin is injected into a vein.

The addicts injecting heroin often have marks all over their bodies. They will start by injecting into the veins of the arm, but the veins there collapse easily. When injecting becomes impossible, the addict moves on to another part of the body.

HEROIN

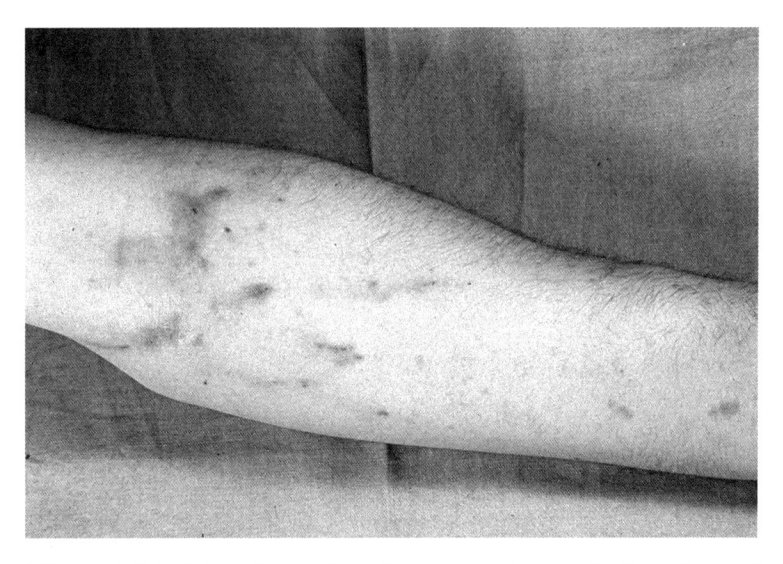

Where addicts inject themselves they cause damage to the veins and skin, often leaving "track marks." These are scars from continuous damage.

Those who are seriously addicted to heroin will also inject their feet, neck, and legs.

When syringes and needles are scarce, an addict trying to get heroin into a vein will resort to the use of blunt or rusty needles. These needles can gash the skin badly. The risk of serious infection from this type of activity is high.

So why do those dependent on heroin continue to inject, when it is the most dangerous, and for most people, the most disgusting way to take the drug? The answer is injecting is a much faster way for heroin to reach the brain and users enjoy the injection ritual.

Wheeling and dealing

In most U.S. cities heroin is traded on the streets, in parks, or from parked cars. However, semipublic places like bars, clubs, and dark alleys are also likely places. Many transactions, whether with a dealer or a user, take place, too, behind the closed doors of "safe" apartments and houses. Locations are passed along the junkies' grapevine.

Small dealers are almost always addicted to heroin themselves. Most of the profit they make goes straight up their nose or into their arms in the form of heroin or other drugs.

HEROIN ON THE STREETS

Those on the fringes of dealing will act as "runners," meaning they ferry drugs from place to place. They might also keep drugs for dealers who are under surveillance by the police.

Dealers, of course, act outside the law by selling an illegal drug like heroin. However, dependence on illegal drugs often leads to other criminal activities, because addicts often have no other way of finding the money to pay for their addiction. No drug causes crime, but users are involved in a high number of crimes in cities like New York and Washington, D.C., London and Liverpool, Sydney and Hong Kong. In New York, studies show that more than one-fourth of all street crime is committed by heroin users.

> *Small dealers are almost always addicted to heroin themselves. Most of the profit they make goes straight up their nose or into their arms in the form of heroin or other drugs.*

Washington, D.C. has a serious problem with violent crime, linked to drugs like heroin and the cocaine derivative, crack. There was nearly one murder a day in 1988, and the number rose in 1989. Burglaries and car thefts are rising, even in once- "safe" middle-class areas. The police are finding it hard to control the drug gangs. There has even been a proposal to impose the extreme measure of a curfew, whereby no one under the age of 18 would be allowed out between 11 p.m. and 6 a.m. during the week and between midnight and 6 a.m. on weekends.

> *A once-wealthy Hollywood antique dealer was sent to prison in 1984 for staging 64 bank robberies to pay for heroin. His addiction was costing him $800 a day.*

Even the apparently respectable citizen who gets caught in addiction can turn to crime. A once-wealthy Hollywood antique dealer was sent to prison in 1984 for staging 64 bank robberies to pay for heroin. His addiction was costing him $800 a day.

Most research, though, suggests that people become involved in crime first and heroin second. It may be that a successful crime leads to a heroin-user buying, and using, a

HEROIN

To help the fight against drug smuggling, Britain's Customs and Excise department have acquired some fast inflatable boats.

larger quantity of the drug than they would normally. Heroin on the streets might not cause crime, but it does go hand in hand with it. When heroin takes hold of a community, crime and violence rise, and people start to live in fear.

Most dealers use the latest technology to keep in touch with their own suppliers and those they sell heroin to. In the past, they have used electronic paging devices, or "beepers," to conduct their business. Today, they use portable telephones to keep mobile, carrying out deals on the move to try to stay one step ahead of the law and avoid arrest. It is hard, though not impossible, for police to tap these phones, and this provides another boost for the dealer selling his addictive, often deadly, product.

8

THE COST TO HEALTH

Those abusing heroin suffer from general ill-health and a wide range of diseases. These include some conditions that are not too serious, such as constipation and associated "piles," or hemorrhoids. They also include serious infections, such as the AIDS virus. Heroin addicts are statistically much more likely to become seriously ill or die at an early age than those who do not use drugs.

Overdose

Every year, two out of every 100 users of heroin will die. Most deaths will be sudden and many, perhaps one in three, will have been caused by an overdose. Some heroin abusers overdose on purpose, in desperation or as a cry for help. Many, though, do it unintentionally.

When someone takes an overdose, the part of the brain that controls breathing is harmed, and the overdose victim suffocates. Overdosing may stop short of being fatal and may mean blackouts and long-lasting effects. Drug abusers sometimes report that they have given other abusers CPR to keep them breathing.

> *Every year, two out of every 100 users of heroin will die.*

How much heroin constitutes a lethal overdose varies from one individual to another. Those who have been using heroin for a long time, who have a high tolerance, can be killed by taking a dose of heroin that is more pure than they are used to.

HEROIN

Addicts might become desperate for heroin and forget about the dangers, or they may not know about them.

Often the cause of death is an overdose from a mixture of heroin and other opiate drugs, like the heroin substitute methadone, with common painkillers like codeine. Commonly prescribed drugs, especially barbituates, can also be fatal when mixed with heroin.

Infections

Heroin addicts often have skin conditions because they inject themselves, sometimes not very well, with substances that the body is not used to. If users miss a vein, they can get enormous swellings that may last for many months. Sometimes, the skin above the injection will form an ulcer, called a "burn" by addicts. Skin infections also develop because the conditions in which addicts inject themselves are unhygienic. These infections can usually be treated with antibiotics but addicts tend to ignore them until they become serious.

Drug addicts often suffer from ill health and skin conditions. Some of the substances with which the drugs are mixed cause ulcers and even gangrene.

THE COST TO HEALTH

Swollen and scarred hands can result from frequent injections. If the user misses a vein the swelling that results may last for several months.

Sometimes addicts get gangrene after a severe reaction to the substances mixed into street heroin, and addicts may need to have legs and fingers amputated. A common problem is blood infection, which may lead to infection of the lining of the heart.

The way heroin is abused, often among a small group of people sharing needles, means that epidemics, large and small, are commonplace. A number of diseases are known to spread easily among heroin addicts. A type of yeast, Candida albicans, which causes the disease often known as thrush, has caused fevers, chills, and sickness among heroin abusers. It has also been found to cause an eye disease that can cause blindness. Other infections found more commonly among heroin addicts are tetanus, tuberculosis, and malaria.

Hepatitis

One of the most infective viruses known is hepatitis B. It is the commonest cause of inflammation of the liver among those injecting heroin. In one study, eight out of 10 drug abusers had been infected by hepatitis B. The virus can cause stomach pain, feelings of sickness, and general ill-health as well as the characteristic yellowy eyes of jaundice.

HEROIN

However, many people in the early stages of a hepatitis infection do not show symptoms. A few of those infected will become exhausted, vomit, and become confused and irritable; eventually their livers fail and they die. A small proportion of others develop liver cancer.

Most people who contract hepatitis B suffer only a series of minor symptoms, especially a flulike illness, and are likely to suffer from liver damage. Those infected will continue to pass on the disease to sexual partners and, in the case of women, to children born to them.

Heroin abusers are also at risk of infection from other hepatitis viruses about which little is known. These viruses cause liver damage in up to half of those infected.

AIDS

AIDS, the Acquired Immune Deficiency Syndrome, is now the most serious disease found among needle-sharing drug abusers. Over the next decade, it is likely to cause a dramatic increase in the death rates of those using heroin. AIDS is thought to be caused by the human immunodeficiency virus, HIV, which causes a breakdown in the body's ability to resist disease. HIV is found in tears, saliva, urine, breast milk, blood, and other body fluids. The spread of the resulting AIDS virus has been surprisingly rapid in New York City. Injecting now accounts for about one in three AIDS cases in New York. Edinburgh, Scotland, where heroin is commonly injected as well, has also experienced high numbers of AIDS cases.

> *The spread of the AIDS virus has been rapid in New York City. Edinburgh, Scotland, where heroin is commonly injected as well, has also experienced high numbers of AIDS cases.*

AIDS is spread by unprotected sexual contact, so addicts can pass it to non-drug using partners. It is also spread through contaminated needles and syringes which, because needles are in short supply, are often passed on from abuser to abuser. Frequently someone infected by the HIV virus will have no symptoms for many years, so there is no way of knowing for sure if an apparently healthy heroin abuser is infected unless he or she takes a test for antibodies to the HIV virus.

THE COST TO HEALTH

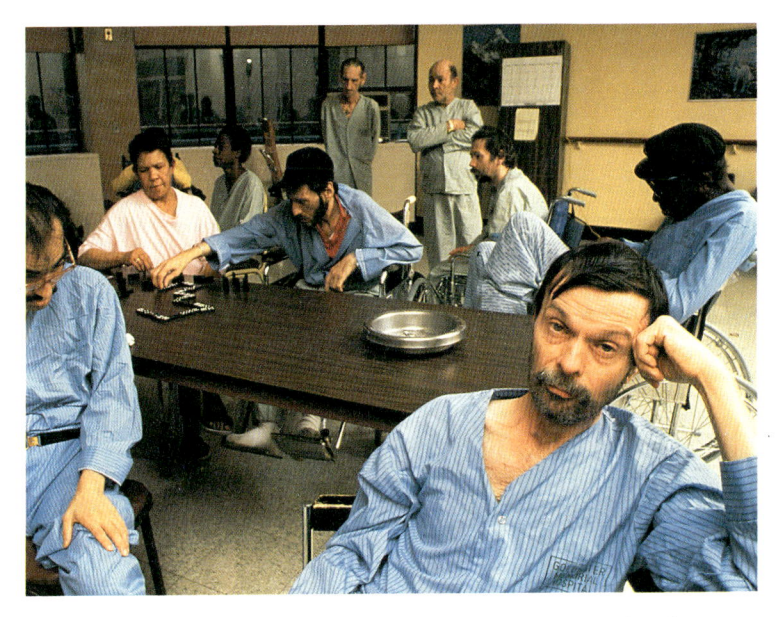

Many of these AIDS victims in a New York hospital are also drug addicts. The HIV virus that causes AIDS is transmitted by sharing needles for injections. Addiction weakens the immune system and makes the addict more likely to get AIDS.

AIDS is frighteningly common among users who inject heroin. Studies show that more than half of those injecting the drug are infected. It is too early to know whether all those infected with the HIV virus will die from AIDS, though it looks increasingly unlikely that large numbers of infected people will be able to fight off the disease.

The lifestyle of drug abusers means that they may be more likely than other HIV-positive people to develop AIDS. Continued injecting and constant infection weakens the immune system, as does heavy drinking, anxiety and depression, and liver damage — all of which are common among abusers. In Europe the number of cases of AIDS among drug abusers has multiplied more than ten times since 1984. One in five currently has AIDS, and the numbers are climbing.

In New York, drug abuse is rampant in poor areas of the city, where the recorded increases of AIDS are growing fastest. In one area alone, the number of cases nearly doubled between 1986 and 1987. Current estimates are that more than 100,000 drug abusers in the city are infected with the virus. An addict's chance of being exposed to HIV increases each time he injects.

HEROIN

Sick in mind and body

Heroin abuse can affect people in many ways, both physically and mentally. Users usually eat very poorly, preferring to spend what money they have on the drug. The abuser may just eat cookies, candy, and junk food, and this leads to malnourishment. Vitamin deficiencies may make drug abusers even more likely to suffer from infections.

Heroin depresses breathing, sometimes dangerously, but it also reduces the addicts' ability to cough efficiently. Fluid that would normally be coughed up collects in the lungs, and this can lead to bronchitis and pneumonia.

Heroin also reduces both male and female fertility. However, it is possible for women to become pregnant while taking the drug. Women who do conceive run a high risk of having a smaller baby than normal, which will have to be helped to breathe in an incubator. The growth of such babies is often restricted, and they have lower-than-average rates of survival.

> The abuse of heroin is also a major cause of mental illness. Depression afflicts one in six heroin abusers, and one in three of those trying to give up the drug.

Female heroin abusers often have twins or triplets, and statistics show there may be a slightly increased risk of the baby being deformed. Repeated use of heroin during pregnancy leads to a baby being born physically addicted to the drug. Babies born addicted are restless and irritable, squirming and moving a lot. In extreme cases they may suffer convulsions or die.

The abuse of heroin is also a major cause of mental and emotional disturbance. Depression afflicts one in six heroin abusers, and one in three of those trying to give up the drug. Heroin can also cause frightening hallucinations, both seeing and hearing things that are not really there.

The physical and mental stresses are a high price to pay for the addict, who may risk losing friends and family. It is often necessary for everyone concerned to seek help from outside. Addicts may know that what they are doing is wrong, but they often cannot and will not help themselves. Usually, the addict will lament: "It makes you sick. I vomited all the time, but I kept taking it. You know it's wrong, but you keep using it."

9

THE SOCIAL COSTS

Heroin does not only affect the individual who abuses it. Addiction to heroin can have devastating effects on both the families and friends of addicts. It affects whole communities, where widespread drug abuse may leave a mess of discarded and dangerous drug paraphernalia, as well as vomit. It turns communities into places where fear of addicts, especially among older people, may be common, and where people who protest to or about users or dealers may be violently threatened, assaulted, or killed.

Society has to pay financially to reduce drug problems, too. Money has to be found for customs officials and equipment to deter traffickers, for enforcement of drug laws, and for help and treatment for those who want to stop their dependence on drugs.

> *"You don't care about anybody. It affects your family. It affects people who don't even take it."*

There are other social consequences. Regular heroin abusers may not be able to hold down a job, because of their need to obtain supplies of the drug. Even if the user does find a job, it may not pay well enough for the user to pay for his or her habit. The obsession with obtaining a fix often leads to fights within the family, and between the heroin abuser and his or her partner. One user describes how heroin affects everyday life: "You don't care about anybody. It affects your family. It affects people who don't even take it." It can also cause friction between friends: "I've known really good guys change

HEROIN

completely. You can't trust anyone, there's no such thing as friendship."

Heroin addicts who used to have a stable lifestyle can find themselves increasingly isolated. They associate only with other addicts, as the consequences of their addiction become unacceptable to employers, friends, and families.

Self-help

Drug users who realize what their addiction is doing to them may try to stop using drugs. Some will stop using drugs suddenly and experience the withdrawal symptoms, which are similar to a bad case of the flu, known as "cold turkey." "You sweat, you get diarrhea, and you don't feel like eating for a few days, but after that it's all right." Others may substitute other drugs, such as methadone, for heroin and try to cut down their intake more slowly. Some users may move, perhaps to another state, to get away from the drug scene.

> *"You sweat, you get diarrhea, and you don't feel like eating for a few days, but after that it's all right."*

Many drug users do manage to break their habit for many years at a time, and sometimes forever. One ex-addict admits: "Staying off's the hard part. I didn't see any point in going to a doctor. I just did it on my own." There are, however, those whose attempts to stop do not last very long. Heroin addicts often see such failures as a personal weakness rather than an addictive effect of the drug, and they may start to see themselves as failures with no hope of a way out.

> *"Staying off's the hard part. I didn't see any point in going to a doctor. I just did it on my own."*

This can result in the addicts feeling intense hatred toward themselves. They can become angry and aggressive toward others, especially those closest to them. They may shout, abuse, and hit those around them. If the drug taker has a spouse or children, they may be battered. This, in turn, may

THE SOCIAL COSTS

make the drug taker hate himself or herself more and lead to a condition of deep depression.

The self-hatred can also lead to addicts cutting themselves with knives and razors, taking overdoses on purpose, and trying to blot out the bad things in their lives with more heroin. It becomes a downward spiral. Disastrous crises become a part of normal life. A heroin abuser may start to take regular overdoses, even twice a week.

New trends

Because of the headline-grabbing attention given to crack, heroin-related topics have been pushed off the front page. However, this trend may change. World production of heroin has increased and it has become much purer, thus enabling the user to smoke rather than inject it. Purer, smokable heroin is readily available on the streets of New York, San Francisco, and other big cities, and may revolutionize the heroin trade by expanding the market to new groups of users.

Some users of cocaine and crack have avoided heroin

As part of a program to stop drug trafficking, a plainclothes policeman talks to worried parents in an inner-city area with a growing drug problem.

47

HEROIN

because of the fear of needles and fear of possibly being exposed to the AIDS virus. After the initial crack high, which generally lasts only a few minutes, a crack user is desperate to avoid the following severe depression. Smokable heroin may be used to ease the crash. Suburban teens, whose drug of choice has traditionally been beer, may also find smokable heroin appealing. A $10 bag of smokable heroin is a more affordable drug for both the young and the poor.

In the Mott Haven section of the South Bronx, New York, an area known for wholesale drug trade, dealers from all over

> Overdoses from the drug "Tango & Cash"... resulted in the deaths of twelve people and the hospitalization of 130 others.

the Northeast come to buy bags of heroin. On February 1, 1991, there was a rush of activity in emergency rooms throughout the Bronx, Newark (New Jersey), and Hartford (Connecticut). Overdoses from the drug "Tango & Cash" (a derivative of fentanyl, a potent tranquilizer) resulted in the deaths of twelve people and the hospitalization of 130 others. Fentanyl, which originated on the West Coast, has been linked to 100 deaths in California. Fentanyl may have come east as a "designer," or concocted, substitute for heroin, and in reponse to the constant demand for drugs.

Action

Sometimes parents, friends, and relatives of drug addicts decide to do something about the problem of heroin abuse. At its most dramatic, this would be in the form of a protest march on the projects or streets where dealers sell heroin. Action like this has happened in both New York City and Belfast, Northern Ireland.

A quieter approach has been adopted in north London. When Anne's 18-year-old daughter died because she had used heroin, Anne discovered that the children of some of her closest friends had also fallen victim to the drug and its effects.

The parents decided to get together and secretly gather information about the drug dealers who were supplying the young people in their community. They pieced the information together by watching where those taking drugs went, by

THE SOCIAL COSTS

Protest marches against drugs have been organized in many large cities. These protesters in New York are anxious to make everyone aware that action must be taken. Areas with many drug dealers often become violent and dangerous places to live.

listening to what they said, and noting what other people said. By doing this, they faced being beaten up, or even worse, by the dealers.

The picture resulting from this jigsaw of clues was that of a network of runners who carried packages of drugs all over the community, and a number of addresses where drugs were sold or used. The result of the parents' efforts was that more than 20 heroin dealers were arrested and charged.

The activities of the big drug traffickers have been the focus for a great deal of political and public concern. Their power is immense. They are often wealthy and are careful to separate themselves from the riskier parts of the drug trade, so they get caught much less often than smaller user-dealers. They keep their power by being prepared to use violence against both people and property in a ruthless manner, inspiring fear in those who cross them.

49

10

KICKING THE HABIT

The nature of addiction to heroin means that it is difficult for an addict to kick the habit. Heroin provides many drug users with a way to temporarily blot out a miserable world. Giving up heroin involves uncomfortable withdrawal symptoms, although these are not as bad as many addicts imagine, and are certainly unlike the withdrawal scenes shown in some films. Withdrawal symptoms mainly affect the mind, but the physical symptoms are many and include diarrhea, a runny nose, sweating, anxiety, sleeplessness, and stomach pains.

> *There is no magic cure for heroin in a tablet that a doctor can prescribe, though there are some drugs that can help relieve some of the withdrawal symptoms.*

Many addicts, however, remain dependent on heroin because the reasons that they had when they started using the drug have not gone away. For treatment to be effective, it must also look at why drug abusers take heroin in the first place. Many addicts do defeat their habit, sometimes after many tries and sometimes not forever. If a drug abuser cannot stop on his or her own, he or she will need help from different people, who might include family, friends, teachers, doctors, and social workers.

Medical help

Doctors are often the people that addicts turn to when they say they want to give up. In fact they may just be wanting to obtain more drugs. There is no magic cure for heroin in a tablet that a

KICKING THE HABIT

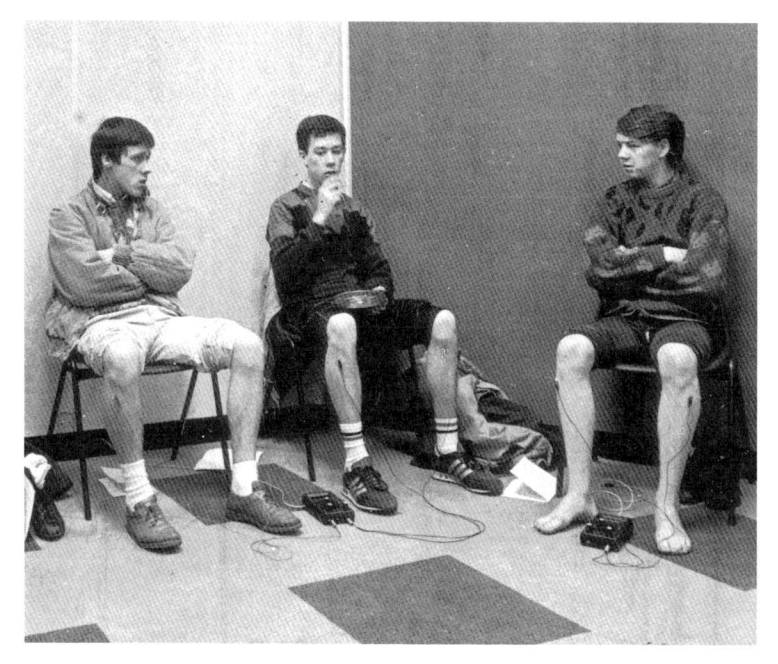

Giving up heroin produces withdrawal symptoms, which make the experience uncomfortable. Different methods for helping the addicts have been tried, one of which is acupuncture.

doctor can prescribe, though there are some drugs that can help relieve some of the withdrawal symptoms.

For many years, treatment with methadone has been one of the standard treatments. Methadone satisfies the craving for heroin, but does not cause the person to feel "high." It can be used in the short term — over a period of days, or at most weeks — to help a heroin abuser switch to a legal supply of drugs and to avoid the worst effects of the withdrawal syndrome. However, this often fails and the addict returns to heroin.

Methadone can also be used in the long term, as an alternative to illegal heroin. The problem has been that addicts sell their methadone on the black market to buy the heroin they prefer. If efforts are made to change the mental and social pressures that started the addiction in the first place, however, long-term "maintenance" treatment with methadone can be successful. Critics still argue though that long-term treatment with methadone, which is as addicting as heroin, is a way of merely substituting one addiction for another.

HEROIN

Naltrexone is a drug that blocks the euphoric effects of heroin and other opiate drugs, though it does not stop the addicts from experiencing a craving for drugs. It seems to be a useful way of discouraging spur of the moment use of narcotic drugs like heroin, and such impulsive use is considered an important cause of addicts failing to kick their habit. The drug, however, can only work if it is taken; addicts have pretended to take naltrexone without doing so and taken heroin instead.

One way to make certain that it works is to ask a family member, or a girlfriend or boyfriend, to make sure that the drug taker swallows the naltrexone every day. Using the family in treatment like this can be a great help for some addicts.

Nonmedical help

There are organizations modeled on Alcoholics Anonymous, such as Narcotics Anonymous, that are self-help groups for heroin addicts. They act as support groups for those wanting to kick the heroin habit. They involve addicts talking about their addictions openly and discussing how they have overcome particular problems. However, the semireligious atmosphere of some of these groups is not helpful for all addicts. There are also associated groups for the families of addicts, one of which is called Nar-Anon.

Outpatient programs give advice on practical problems like housing and employment, give information and advice on drug problems, and give long-term counseling and advice. They also provide drug-free daytime activities for addicts, and the time and professional advice needed on what more can be done for an addict. Critics note the main problem with these organizations is that when addicts are not attending the programs, they can still obtain drugs if they want to.

> ... addicts may be challenged to become angry and show their emotions which, it is claimed, have been hidden by heroin.

Rehabilitation centers do provide 24-hour care for the addict. These centers are often sited away from easily accessible drugs, and addicts may not be allowed off the grounds at first. Residents are kept busy working in gardens or workshops, cooking and cleaning, and in leisure activities.

KICKING THE HABIT

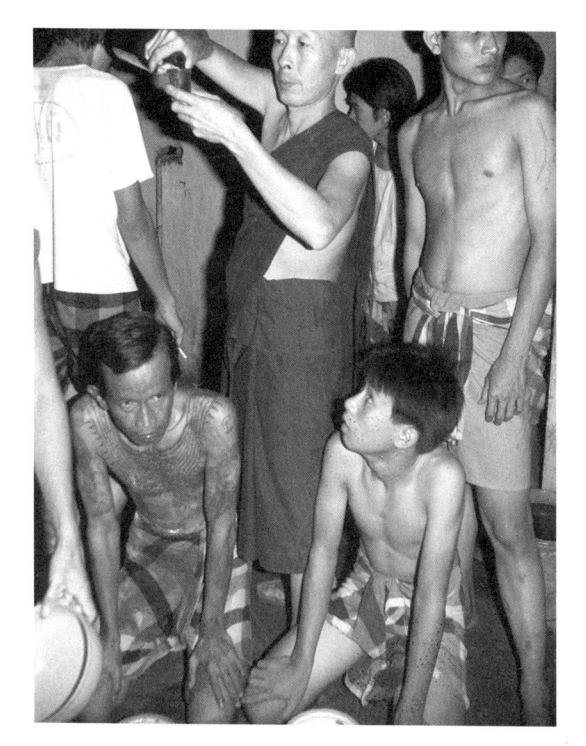

In this drug rehabilitation center in Thailand, addicts support each other through their withdrawal period. Bark medicine is given to help alleviate the symptoms.

Some centers offer general support and counseling, while others have their own individual philosophies. At some centers, addicts may be challenged to become angry and show their emotions which, it is claimed, have been hidden by heroin. Other houses may be run on religious lines. Unfortunately there are very few openings available at any of these centers, and there is a high dropout rate.

The alternatives to these residential programs are few but can be effective. Rehabilitation in the community is sometimes achieved through the work of probation officers, nurses, doctors, and social workers. They can provide skilled support for those trying to stay off heroin.

There are several forms of therapy that can be given to support an addict who is trying to "kick the habit." Group therapy sessions can be a useful way for heroin abusers to learn, for example, how to reduce the craving for drugs, and how to gradually reduce the amount of drugs they take.

HEROIN

Family tensions and disputes can be part of the reason for addiction, so family therapy can sometimes help. This sort of therapy is used to help family members learn to free themselves from codependency, so that they no longer give the addict covert encouragement to keep taking drugs.

> *Family tensions and disputes can be part of the reason for addiction, so family therapy can sometimes help.*

Therapy is frequently used to help the heroin addict identify the things that influence his or her drug taking. When this has been achieved, the addict is then encouraged to develop ways of coping with the influences so that they can be avoided in the future.

Try, try, and try again

Carol had been using heroin for two years and was spending more and more money on the drug. She had had difficulty settling in the city where her husband worked, and their marriage was on the verge of breaking up. She was thin and was feeling depressed. She started on a detoxification program of methadone, gradually reducing the dose.

Initially all went well, but then Carol started to miss appointments at the clinic she was attending and eventually started to use heroin again, dropping out of treatment altogether. After a while, she returned to the clinic and again did well on methadone. This time, however, she was prepared to examine the reasons why she took heroin. She moved back to a town nearer her family home and, with the help of her husband who returned with her, remained drug free for several years.

Carol had started to use heroin to avoid conflict with her husband. She had been missing her parents and the places where she had been brought up. She also felt depressed because her husband had a good job and she did not. When she began to realize where the problem lay, she was better prepared to give up heroin.

11

WAR ON HEROIN

Despite widespread concern about the effects of heroin, both on individuals and on society as a whole, the drug continues to be available on the streets of most major cities. Over the years, the price of heroin has fallen steadily while its purity has tended to increase. The problem for the health of society is that heroin is enormously profitable. Sales in the U.S. alone total more than the combined profits of the top 500 U.S. corporations, and more than the budgets of many developing countries.

> The problem for the health of society is that heroin is enormously profitable.

Profits can be made on relatively small-scale smuggling. For example, the amount of illegal heroin that supplies the U.K. for one day would fit into a single shopping bag. The smuggling is highly organized, and activities against it are discouraged by threatened and actual violence. Life is cheap and murder common among the drug traffickers.

Efforts to bring the drug problem under control are continually being mounted. These are aimed at all stages of heroin production, from the start of the chain in the countries that grow the opium poppy, to the end of the chain where the small-time dealer sells a bag of the drug to another addict.

The growing countries

Clearly breaking the supply chain at the source is an attractive option in the battle against heroin. Blocking production would

HEROIN

slow the stream of heroin that is exported all over the world. However, it is not an easy option to implement. Illicit opium is grown in areas and countries that are often politically unstable and economically weak. Profits from drugs are often used to prop up a government or to weaken it if it is threatening to crack down on producers.

One way of stopping opium production is to burn or spray the growing opium poppies. The problem with this strategy is that the key areas are controlled by bandits or antigovernment forces. A second way, which suffers from the same limitations, is to give aid to the police and antidrug agencies in the growing countries. A third approach is to encourage farmers to grow other crops like sugar beets, fruit, or grain, and help them in this by building roads and subsidizing their work.

> *Blocking production would slow the stream of heroin that is exported all over the world. However, it is not an easy option.*

There are many obstacles. Armed bandits, private armies, and bands of guerrillas run unchecked by police and other law enforcement officers. In this situation taking any action is difficult and dangerous. Action by teams of officials from Western governments can give rise to anti-Western feeling and unite a community against the attempts to cut opium production.

In Thailand, for example, anti-opium projects have been given support by the United Nations, the U.S., Germany, Australia, Canada, and the Netherlands. The King of Thailand has given his personal backing to the attempts, but results have not been spectacular. There is massive corruption, and the main opium-growing area is controlled by bandits.

However, there have been some successes in programs to replace opium with other crops. Perhaps the most impressive is China, which had an extensive problem of opium addiction. Now other crops have replaced the opium poppy, and opium addiction is no longer common. Yugoslavia, too, has encouraged the planting of other crops and cut out opium-growing. The amount of heroin produced in Pakistan has been reduced, and crop eradication and substitution programs can take much of the credit. Hundreds of pounds of opium have been destroyed there recently.

WAR ON HEROIN

The smugglers

The next stage is the illegal movement of heroin to the country where it is to be distributed. The route is not necessarily direct, in order to try and fool customs authorities. In 1988, in Thailand, more than a ton of heroin was seized — then the world's biggest haul of heroin. It was discovered by accident when the bales of rubber it was hidden in were exposed to the rain. It had been destined first for New York, and then probably for distribution throughout the U.S. and Europe. It is thought that the American Mafia was behind the shipment.

> Drugs have been found inside hollowed-out pineapples, in the false bottoms of suitcases, and in the stomachs of smugglers, swallowed in plastic bags or condoms . . .

In another seizure, this time at London's Heathrow airport, heroin was disguised as candy, in genuine-looking colored wrappers, packaged in small bags. This seizure was made by chance during a routine inspection. Drugs have been found inside hollowed-out pineapples, in the false bottoms of suitcases, and in the stomachs of smugglers, swallowed in plastic bags or condoms, a very dangerous practice.

This sandal has a carefully hollowed-out sole so that heroin can be smuggled inside it.

HEROIN

An X ray of the stomach of a suspected drug smuggler revealed a pile of nearly 100 condoms containing heroin. The smuggler risks death if one of these parcels should break in his stomach.

The smugglers come from all walks of life, from poor peasant to rich jet-setter. They include professional criminals who smuggle drugs regularly, and "respectable" business people who smuggle on a one-time basis, apparently for the excitement. In addition to these couriers, the traffickers use the huge international movement of cars and trucks, ships, aircraft, and the postal service.

The professional courier will be paid $3,000 to $5,000 for each trip and, passing through the busy airports around the world, is unlikely to be searched unless there has been a tip-off, or he or she appears unduly suspicious. At JFK airport in New York, which handles 30 million passengers a year, as few as one in 100 people are searched or questioned. Customs officials throughout the world believe that they intercept less than 10 percent of the heroin smuggled.

Fighting the war

While as much as 80 percent of drugs seized are caught as a result of random searches, customs officials work in other ways to gather information about traffickers and trafficking. This

WAR ON HEROIN

information-gathering operation is international and can, on occasion, lead to spectacular success in actions taken against drug-smuggling rings.

Many countries have specialized drug units that deal with more serious cases, and it may be these units or specialized information-gathering forces that piece together material about drug dealing.

However, international cooperation between officials lags behind the international links of the drug-trade criminals. It is sometimes difficult for the U.S. government to obtain cooperation on a national level from its 14 agencies, which range from the Federal Bureau of Investigation (FBI) to the Drug Enforcement Agency (DEA) to the Coast Guard and customs officials.

Drug dealers are ruthlessly determined to preserve the profits they receive from drugs. They have the best boats and planes for their smuggling operations. By contrast, customs officials often have outdated equipment. It frequently seems an unequal contest. Sometimes police and customs will allow drugs to pass through a port or airport in an attempt to identify who is involved in the smuggling.

> ... in places like New York City, where drug use has reached epidemic proportions, the courts simply cannot cope. The jails are full, so most of the dealers convicted are given small fines and go straight back to dealing.

In some areas of the world, the authorities are successful in arresting and charging the small and medium-sized drug dealers. Yet, in places like New York City, where drug use has reached epidemic proportions, the courts simply cannot cope. The jails are full, so most of the dealers convicted are given small fines and go straight back to dealing.

The large drug dealers are careful to cover their tracks. They usually pass, or "launder," their money through several bank accounts in out-of-the-way places so that the connection between them and heroin cannot be proved: "A man walks into a shop with $1 million in New York. The same day, someone collects the same amount from a shop in Bangkok. Legitimate banks aren't involved and the profits become impossible to trace."

HEROIN

Prevention and cure?

If restricting the amount of heroin that gets onto the streets is an almost impossible task, then perhaps the answer is to restrict demand. To be successful with this, difficult questions about why so many people take heroin must be answered. Some experts have suggested that the structure of the economy of societies should be changed, so that the typical poor, unemployed user of heroin is actually given an opportunity to work for which he or she is paid.

Attempts at prevention have also been seen in health education programs. Some of these programs, however, have been attacked. Critics claim that the people the programs were trying to reach ignored or rejected them because they could not identify with the way in which the programs were advertised. However, peer counseling in schools has proven to be quite effective. Educating the young to the facts about heroin and what it can do has been shown to affect people's attitudes toward the drug.

> "Drug couriers from Pakistan have been caught smuggling heroin disguised as candy. Just one piece could kill a child."

There is much more to stopping heroin abuse than politicians' words about a "war on drugs." The reality is that no one approach on its own is likely to succeed. It is necessary to attack heroin on all fronts, at its production, distribution, and consumption stages. It is important that supply is restricted and at the same time the apparent need that people have for the drug is reduced. Often, it is the innocent that suffer in the deadly chain from producer to user. A customs officer at London's Heathrow airport gave this example of how heroin can threaten the lives of innocent people: "Drug couriers from Pakistan have been caught smuggling heroin disguised as candy. Just one piece could kill a child."

INFORMATION

United States
Center for Science in the Public Interest
1501 16th Street, N.W.
Washington, D.C. 20036

Department of Education
Office of the Secretary
Room 4181
400 Maryland Avenue, S.W.
Washington, D.C. 20202

Narcotics Anonymous U.S.
PO Box 622
Sun Valley, California 91352

National Clearinghouse for Drug Abuse Information
5600 Fishers Lane
Rockville, Maryland 20857

World Service Board of Families Anonymous
Families Anonymous Inc.
Box 528
Van Nuys, California 91408

Nar-Anon
350 W. 5th Street, #207
Palos Verdes Peninsula, CA 90274

Canada
Addiction Research Foundation
33 Russell Street
Toronto, Ontario M5S 2S1

Alberta Alcohol and Drug Abuse Commission
10909 Jasper Avenue, 7th Floor
Edmonton, Alberta, T5J 3M9

INDEX

A
action against drugs 14, 48
addiction 4, 6, 13–14, 22, 29, 30, 32, 45–46, 50, 56
addicts 6, 8, 17, 28–30, 33, 39
Afghanistan 5, 15, 16, 23
AIDS 9, 33, 35, 39, 42–43, 48
alkaloids 4, 21
anti-opium campaign 14, 56
Australia 23, 26, 37, 56

B
bribes 25
British government 13
Burma 5, 16, 18

C
cash crop 17
chemicals 21–22
China 7, 11, 13, 56
climate 15
crime 7, 8, 18, 29, 32–33, 37–38, 56
crop substitution 56
customs 5, 23–25, 45, 57–58
drug units 59

D
dealers 7, 23, 26–28, 36, 38, 48–49, 59
dependency 4, 6, 31, 34–35, 37, 50
detoxification 4, 9, 54
diamorphine 4, 8
drug education 60
Drug Enforcement Agency (DEA) 26, 59
drug lords 18
drug traffickers 17, 18, 45, 49, 58

E
effects of heroin on
  body 9, 30–31, 33, 35, 39, 44
  brain 30–31, 39, 44
  society 45, 55
endorphins 5, 30, 31
Europe 12, 23, 26, 43, 57

G
governments 13–14, 16, 59

H
health risks 9, 22, 35, 40–44
hepatitis 41–42
heroin
  base 4, 22
  cutting 8, 22
  injecting 4, 5, 30, 33–36, 40, 42
  manufacture 5, 7, 18, 22–23
  purity 5, 8–9, 22, 39, 47, 55
  salt 4, 22
  smoking 5, 13, 30, 34
  sniffing 5, 30, 34
  strength 8
  trading 23, 36–38
HIV virus 9, 42, 43

I
infections 40–41, 43, 44
international corporation 14, 59
Iran 16
Italy 27

K
Khun Sa 18

L
Laos 5, 15

INDEX

laudanum 4, 12
"laundering" money 59

M
Mafia 26–27, 57
medical help 50–52
medicine, use of heroin in 8, 10, 12, 18, 21
methadone 46, 51, 54
Mexico 5, 16, 23
morphine 4, 7, 14, 21

N
naltrexone 52
Narcotics Anonymous 9, 52
natural painkillers 4, 5, 30
New York 6, 22, 32–33, 37, 42, 43, 47–48, 57, 58, 59
North America 26

O
opium 4, 5–7, 21
   dens 13, 14
   farmers 16–17, 23
   history of use 7, 10–14
   latex 19, 21
   poppy 5, 7, 10, 15
   production 15, 47, 55–56
Opium Wars 7, 13, 14
organized crime 18, 23–24, 26–27, 49, 56
outpatient programs 52
overdose 8, 12, 39–40, 47, 48

P
painkillers 5, 21, 30
Pakistan 5, 15–16, 23, 56, 60
police 24, 37, 38, 59
poppy 5, 7, 10, 15, 21
   growing 15–16, 18
   harvesting 19–20
   seed capsule 10, 15, 19
   yields 17
profits 16, 17, 22, 27, 55–56, 59

Q
quitting heroin use 9, 46, 50–54

R
reasons for heroin use 8, 9, 28–29, 30, 51, 54, 60
rehabilitation centers 9, 52–54
runners 37, 49

S
satellite photos 15
self-help 46, 52
smuggling 5, 17, 23, 24–26, 55, 57–58

T
"Tango & Cash" 48
Thailand 5, 15, 56–57
therapy 53–54
tolerance 31, 39
treatment 45, 50–54

U
U.K. 13, 24, 28, 34, 37, 55
unemployment 28, 45
U.S. 5, 14, 16, 17, 24, 26, 27, 36, 37, 55, 56, 57, 59
users, profile of 6, 28

V
violence 18, 24, 27, 37, 45, 49, 55–56

W
Washington, D.C. 37
withdrawal symptoms 4, 6, 9, 12, 46, 50
"works" 4, 33
World Health Organization 14, 18

Y
Yugoslavia 56

© Copyright 1992, text, Steck-Vaughn Company

All rights reserved. No reproduction, copy or transmission of this publication may be made without written permission from the publisher.

Library of Congress Cataloging-in-Publication Data

Pownall, Mark.
    Heroin / written by Mark Pownall.
        p. cm. — (Drugs — the complete story)
    Includes index.
    Summary: Presents information on heroin and related substances and discusses the current social problems connected with use of these drugs.
        ISBN 0-8114-3201-7   —   ISBN 0-8114-3208-4 (soft cover)
    1. Heroin habit — Juvenile literature.   2. Heroin — Juvenile literature.   [1. Heroin.   2. Drug abuse.]   I. Title.   II. Series.
HV5822.H4P69   1991
362.29'3 — dc20   91-26182
                                                                           CIP AC

Consultants: Kenneth J. Schmidt, Passaic County, N.J., Probation Dept.; Marilyn Devroye, consultant for Psychiatric Institutes of America, Washington, DC.

Editors: Margaret Sinclair, Gina Kulch

Cover design by Joyce Spicer

Typeset by Tom Fenton Studio, Neptune, NJ
Printed and bound by Lake Book, Melrose Park, IL

Photographic Credits
Cover: © James Minor, *inset:* © Lefever/Grushow/Grant Heilman, Inc. 6 Don Davis/Tropix; 7 Mary Evans; 2, 9 Christopher Pillitz/Impact Photos; 11 J. Allan Cash; 12 The Trustees of the British Museum; 14 Mary Evans; 3, 16 J. Allan Cash; 17 Griffiths-Magnum; 18 David Browne; 20 a) Associated Press/Topham b)Griffiths-Magnum; 24 Popperfoto; 25 Topham Picture Library; 27 Associated Press/Topham; 29 David Hoffman; 31 David Browne; 3, 33 Associated Press/Topham; 35 David Hoffman; 36 Science Photo Library; 38 Topham Picture Library; 40 Associated Press/Topham; 41 J. Allan Cash; 43 Hank Morgan/Science Photo Library; 47 David Hoffman; 49 David Browne; 51 Peter Marlow/Magnum Photos Inc; 53 Errington/Hutchinson Library; 57 David Hoffman; 58 David Browne.

Original text and illustrations
© Heinemann Educational Books Ltd. 1991